A FOCUS ON...

IMMIGRATION & TOLERANCE

©2018
Book Life
King's Lynn
Norfolk PE30 4LS

ISBN: 9781786372307

Written by:
Charlie Ogden

Edited by:
Kirsty Holmes

Designed by:
Daniel Scase

A catalogue record for this book
is available from the British Library.

CONTENTS

Words that look like **this** are explained in the glossary on **PAGE 31.**

IMMIGRATION

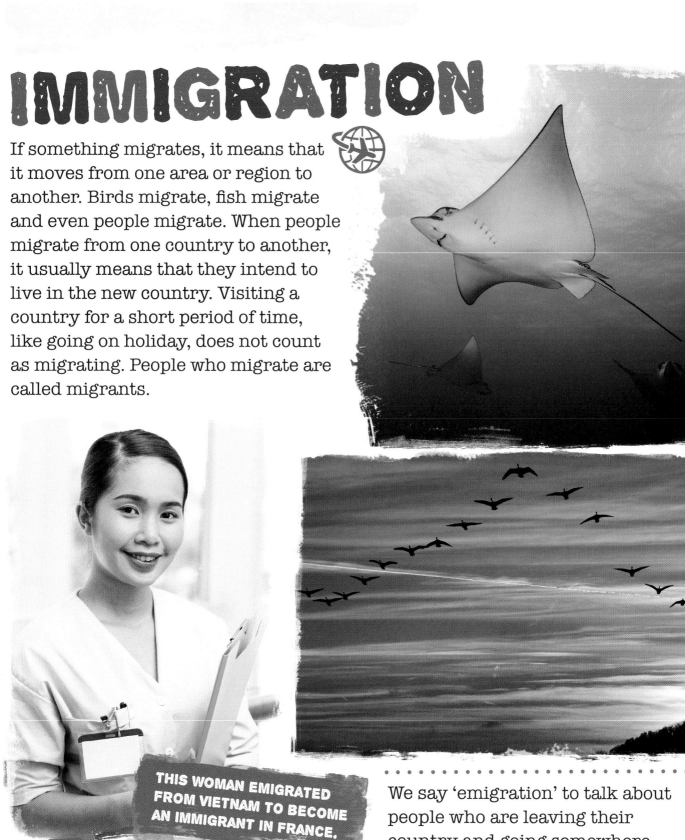

If something migrates, it means that it moves from one area or region to another. Birds migrate, fish migrate and even people migrate. When people migrate from one country to another, it usually means that they intend to live in the new country. Visiting a country for a short period of time, like going on holiday, does not count as migrating. People who migrate are called migrants.

THIS WOMAN EMIGRATED FROM VIETNAM TO BECOME AN IMMIGRANT IN FRANCE.

FRANCE

VIETNAM

We say 'emigration' to talk about people who are leaving their country and going somewhere else. We say 'immigration' to talk about people who are arriving in a new country.

People have been migrating for thousands of years. However, thanks to the **technology** and **transportation** we have today, migrating is easier than ever.

+
0
-
?

This map shows how people migrate to and from different countries. Blue countries have more immigrants entering their country than emigrants leaving it. Orange countries have more emigrants leaving than immigrants entering. Green countries have about the same of each.

Using the map, we can see that countries in North America and Europe receive the most immigrants. Because of this, these countries are home to people from all over the world. We can also see that countries in Africa, South America and Asia receive far less immigrants. This means that fewer people from different countries and backgrounds live in these places.

FACT

THE UNITED STATES OF AMERICA IS HOME TO AROUND 50 MILLION IMMIGRANTS – MORE THAN ANY OTHER COUNTRY IN THE WORLD.

WHY DO PEOPLE
MIGRATE?

There are many different reasons why a person might choose to migrate. These reasons, or factors, can usually be broken down into two groups: 'pull factors' and 'push factors'. Pull factors are reasons for migrating that make a person want to go to a certain country. Push factors are reasons for migrating that make a person want to leave their country.

PULL FACTORS

One of the main pull factors that cause people to immigrate is the chance to have a better job. People move to new countries because they can make more money there, or have a better job. Pull factors like these, are called **economic** pull factors.

PEOPLE OFTEN MIGRATE TO foreign COUNTRIES TO TEACH LANGUAGES.

OTHER PEOPLE MIGRATE TO WEALTHY COUNTRIES TO GET PAID MORE MONEY.

Pull factors that are based around having a better quality of life in a new country are called **social** pull factors. Some people immigrate to countries that have good **services**, such as schools and hospitals. These help people to have a good education and live longer, healthier lives.

Other people move to a new country to be with family and friends who already live there.

Many of the world's wealthiest countries are in North America and Europe. Because of this, there are more opportunities to make money in these places. Also, countries in these regions mostly have strong, stable **governments.** This means that these countries are mostly safe places to live and have good schools and hospitals.

7

PUSH FACTORS

There are many different push factors that can cause a person to emigrate from the country they live in. Most push factors make a person want to leave their country. Stronger push factors can actually force a person to leave their home and their country.

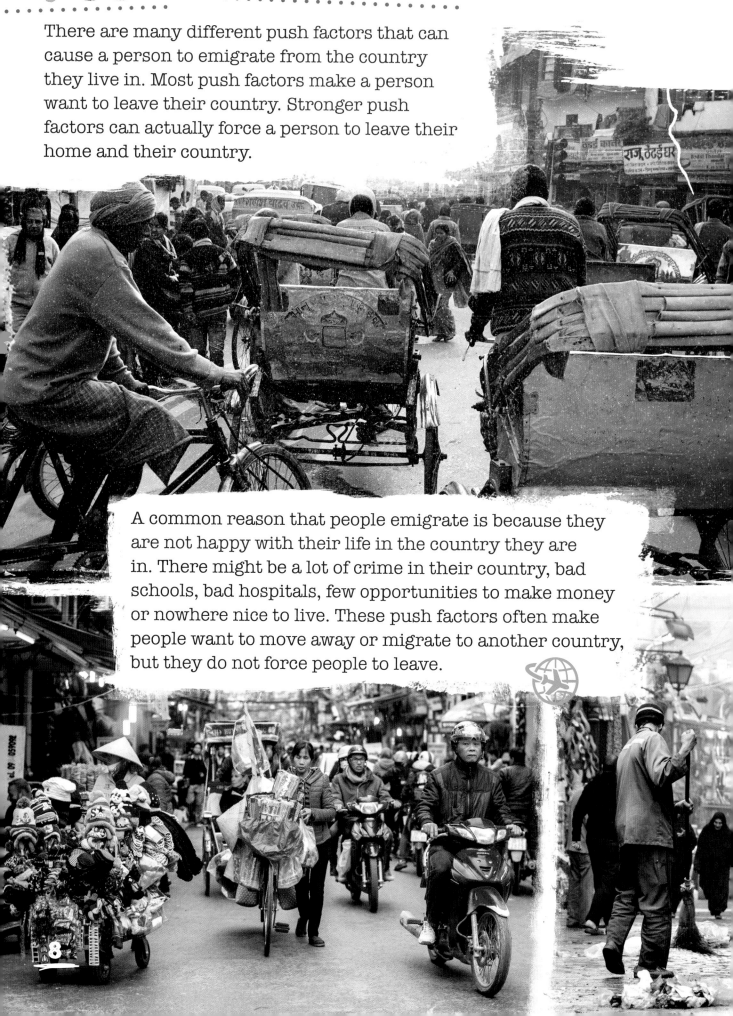

A common reason that people emigrate is because they are not happy with their life in the country they are in. There might be a lot of crime in their country, bad schools, bad hospitals, few opportunities to make money or nowhere nice to live. These push factors often make people want to move away or migrate to another country, but they do not force people to leave.

Some people emigrate to escape persecution. Persecution is when a group of people are mistreated by the people in their country or abused by their government. People might be persecuted for their religion, **race** or **nationality.** In some places, people might be called names, attacked or even thrown in prison just because of the religion they follow. Persecution causes some people to fear for their life. Being part of a group that is being persecuted is a strong push factor and can often cause a person to emigrate from their country.

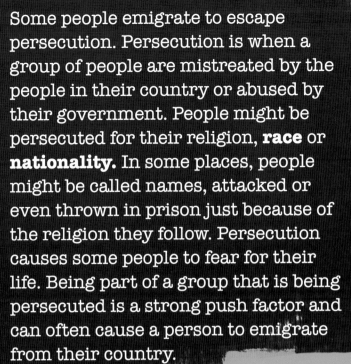

MANY PEOPLE AROUND THE WORLD ARE PERSECUTED FOR THE RELIGION THEY FOLLOW.

The strongest push factors are those that force a person to leave their home and their country. One such push factor is a natural disaster. **Tsunamis** and earthquakes can destroy towns, cities and huge areas of farmland. When natural disasters take place, people are often forced to move to nearby countries that weren't damaged by the disaster.

THIS DAMAGE WAS CAUSED BY A TSUNAMI IN 2011. IT FORCED OVER 200,000 PEOPLE IN JAPAN TO LEAVE THEIR HOMES.

Other natural disasters, such as floods and droughts, can cause a region to run out of **resources**. If a large area of land becomes flooded, the people who live there might be unable to grow food. If a region has a long drought, meaning that it doesn't rain there for a very long time, it may make both food and water difficult to find. In these cases, people are often forced to migrate just to find enough food and water for themselves and their family.

REFUGEES

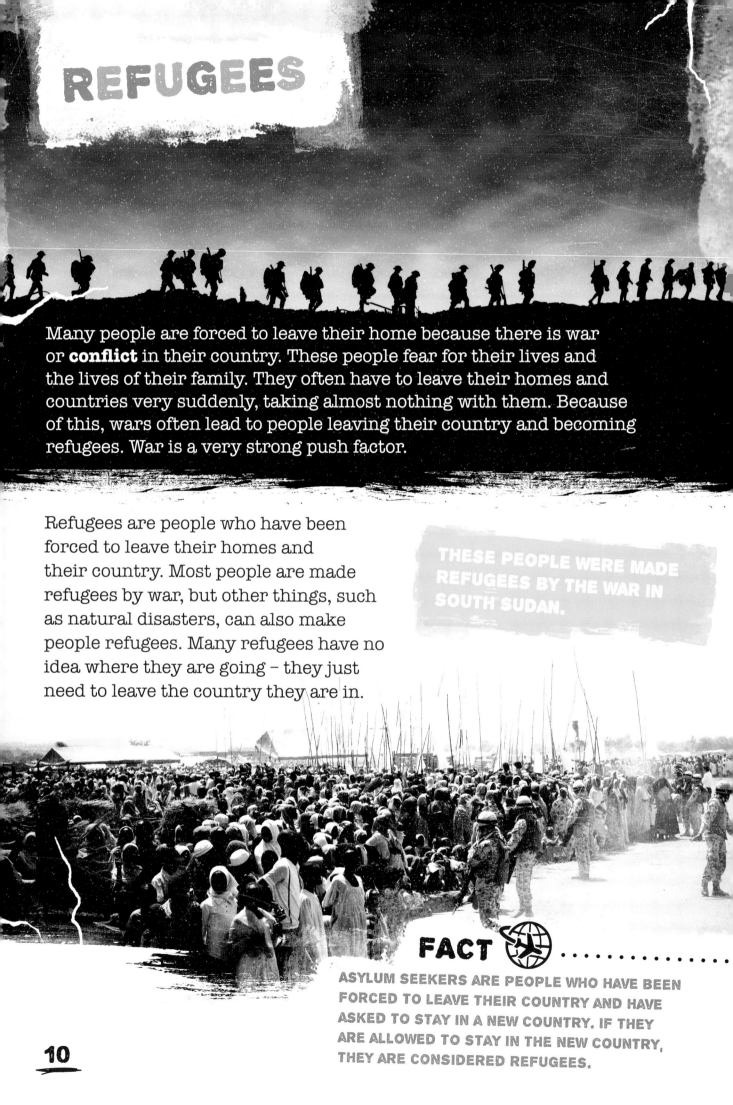

Many people are forced to leave their home because there is war or **conflict** in their country. These people fear for their lives and the lives of their family. They often have to leave their homes and countries very suddenly, taking almost nothing with them. Because of this, wars often lead to people leaving their country and becoming refugees. War is a very strong push factor.

Refugees are people who have been forced to leave their homes and their country. Most people are made refugees by war, but other things, such as natural disasters, can also make people refugees. Many refugees have no idea where they are going – they just need to leave the country they are in.

THESE PEOPLE WERE MADE REFUGEES BY THE WAR IN SOUTH SUDAN.

FACT

ASYLUM SEEKERS ARE PEOPLE WHO HAVE BEEN FORCED TO LEAVE THEIR COUNTRY AND HAVE ASKED TO STAY IN A NEW COUNTRY. IF THEY ARE ALLOWED TO STAY IN THE NEW COUNTRY, THEY ARE CONSIDERED REFUGEES.

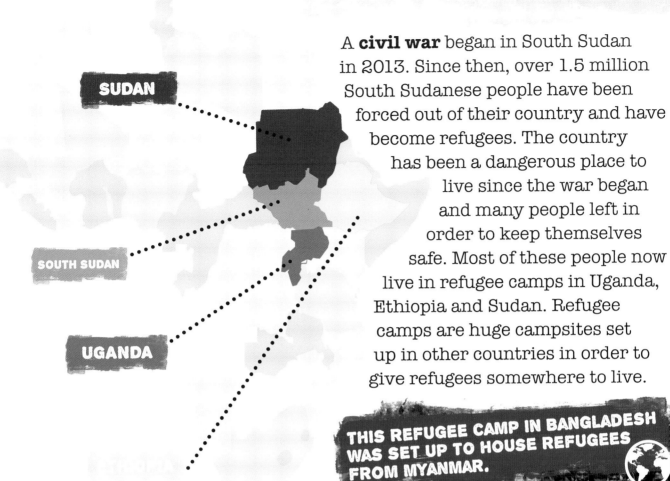

A **civil war** began in South Sudan in 2013. Since then, over 1.5 million South Sudanese people have been forced out of their country and have become refugees. The country has been a dangerous place to live since the war began and many people left in order to keep themselves safe. Most of these people now live in refugee camps in Uganda, Ethiopia and Sudan. Refugee camps are huge campsites set up in other countries in order to give refugees somewhere to live.

SUDAN

SOUTH SUDAN

UGANDA

THIS REFUGEE CAMP IN BANGLADESH WAS SET UP TO HOUSE REFUGEES FROM MYANMAR.

THIS REFUGEE CAMP IN TURKEY WAS SET UP TO HOUSE REFUGEES FROM SYRIA.

Migrating can often be expensive. Without money or help from friends, paying to travel to and live in another country can be difficult. This can make migrating very difficult for refugees. These people often have no family or friends in the country they are traveling to and many of their **possessions** get destroyed as a result of war. Because of this, refugees are often forced to walk many miles, carrying as much as they can on their back, just to escape the persecution or danger in their country. People who were happy and lived comfortable lives can suddenly find themselves becoming refugees, left with very little, and nowhere to go.

BEING AN IMMIGRANT

Being an immigrant can be like stepping into a new world! When people emigrate, they might move to a country which is very different from their own. The people might speak a different language, have a different **culture** and follow different **traditions**. Migrants often have a lot to learn about the countries that they move to.

When people leave their country to become an immigrant somewhere else, they leave behind everything that is familiar to them, like towns and cities, or parts of their lifestyle and culture. For some immigrants, these things might have been part of the reason they wanted to migrate in the first place – they might not have liked their city or lifestyle and this might have pushed them to emigrate. For many others, however, leaving behind the places and things you know can be very upsetting.

TOWNS AND CITIES ARE VERY DIFFERENT FROM ONE ANOTHER. MIGRATING CAN BE CHALLENGING, OR EXCITING!

12

Sometimes migrants emigrate to join friends and family in another country. Others, however, have to leave behind friends and loved ones. Leaving these people behind can be scary and sad. Friends and family support us and make us feel happy and safe, so immigrants often need to make new friends in their new home, and plan to visit their old home if they can.

When a family decides to migrate, they might have to leave some of their possessions behind. This is because transporting all their possessions to their new country would be very expensive. However, this means migrants often have the opportunity to buy new things when they arrive in their new country. Having to leave your possessions behind can be sad, but migrants can create new lives in their new countries.

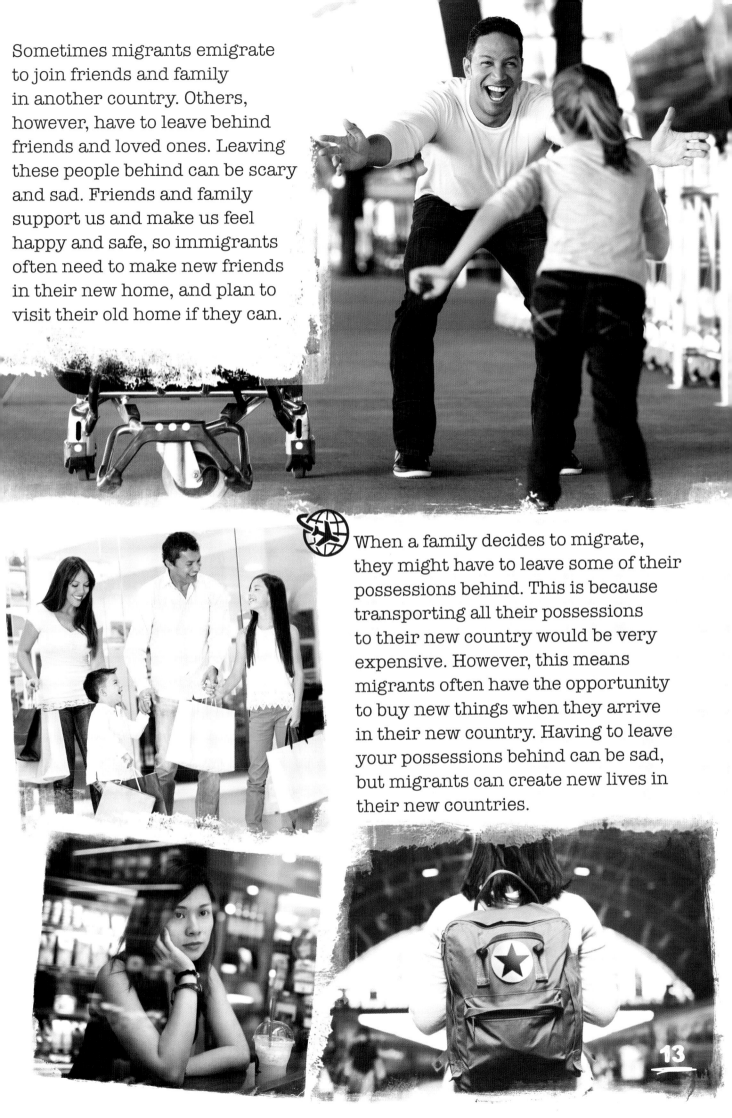

For an immigrant, lots of things about their new country might be very different from their old country. For example, the country's citizens might follow different **laws**. Things that were against the law in their old country might now be okay to do. In the same way, things that used to be legal might now be illegal for them. It is important that people who immigrate learn to live and be happy in their new country.

IN LONDON, PEOPLE CAN CROSS THE STREET WHENEVER AND WHEREVER THEY LIKE. IN NEW YORK, HOWEVER, IT IS ILLEGAL TO CROSS THE ROAD WITHOUT USING A CROSSING POINT.

Many migrants will find that they need to learn a new language in order to understand what people are saying to them and get others to understand what they are saying. They may also have to learn how to live alongside new cultures that they may not have experienced before. It can take time to get used to the differences in a new country, but most migrants are able to live happily alongside the people in their new **community**.

When immigrants arrive in a new country they have to find somewhere to live and work. For immigrants that have family or friends in another country, this might be easier. For refugees that have had to move out of their country very quickly, this might be harder.

Immigrants sometimes have to deal with persecution, mistreatment and racism in their new countries. Racism is when a person is mistreated or persecuted for their race, country or background.

TOLERANCE

Tolerance is when we are fair and welcoming towards people whose opinions, beliefs or culture are different from our own. For example, you and your sibling might want to watch different movies. If you let them choose the movie, even though it is not your favourite, you are being tolerant and welcoming to your sibling's differences. It's important that we show respect and tolerance towards immigrants in order to help them feel welcome.

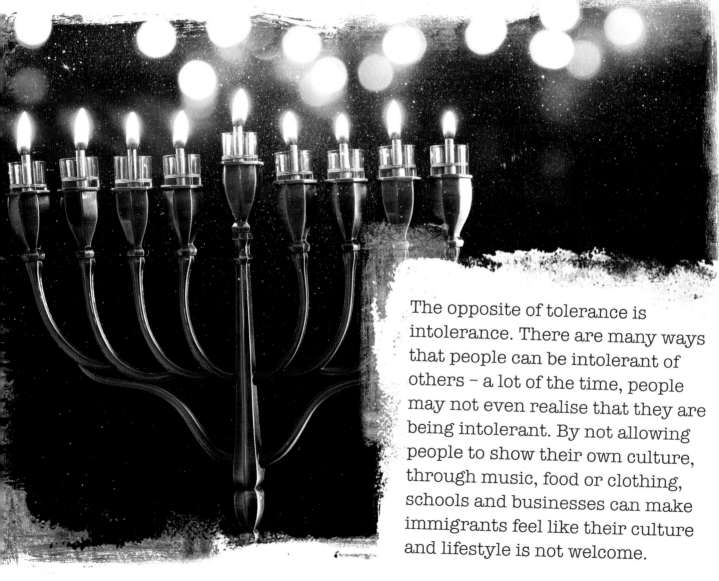

The opposite of tolerance is intolerance. There are many ways that people can be intolerant of others – a lot of the time, people may not even realise that they are being intolerant. By not allowing people to show their own culture, through music, food or clothing, schools and businesses can make immigrants feel like their culture and lifestyle is not welcome.

Intolerance often leads to discrimination. Discrimination is when a person is treated unfairly because of their race, nationality or religion. In many countries, it is illegal to discriminate against someone for these reasons.

People from different cultures might have different lifestyles and beliefs. It's important to remember that, while it might be impossible for everyone to agree about everything, we should all be accepting of other people's cultures and beliefs.

FACT  . . . .

IT'S IMPORTANT THAT SCHOOLS LET CHILDREN CELEBRATE WHATEVER HOLIDAYS ARE IMPORTANT TO THEM AND THEIR CULTURE. THIS SHOWS THAT THE SCHOOL WELCOMES EVERYONE, AND CELEBRATES DIFFERENT CULTURES.

EQUALITY AND DIVERSITY

Immigrants can feel unwelcome in their new community if people don't treat them equally. Immigrant families might have very different lifestyles – they might dress in different clothing, eat different food, listen to different music and speak in a different language. Because people might not understand this, immigrant families can sometimes be made to feel unwelcome by intolerant comments and actions.

EQUALITY

Equality is the idea that all people should be treated the same – that everyone is as important as everyone else and that people should be allowed to choose how they live their lives. To be welcoming to people from other cultures, you have to treat everyone equally.

If a community didn't make sure that immigrant families could get the food they like, or made fun of them for their clothes, they would not be making them feel welcome. They would not be treating them equally – this is intolerance.

Stereotypes can make immigrants feel unwelcome too. A stereotype is a belief that a person holds about someone just because they are part of a certain group of people. For example, it would be a stereotype to believe that someone was good at cooking just because they came from somewhere that is famous for its food, such as Paris. This is a positive stereotype. It assumes something good about the person.

MANY STEREOTYPES ARE BASED ON RELIGION.

Stereotypes cause a problem for immigrants when they become negative. A negative stereotype assumes something bad about the person, just because of where they are from, or their religion. If people believe these things, immigrants may not feel welcome in their new country. It's important that we get to know people for who they are.

Stereotypes assume that everyone from a certain culture, country, race or religion is the same. Because of this, we can say that stereotypes are a kind of discrimination. Stereotypes do not consider people as individuals with their own thoughts, beliefs and actions.

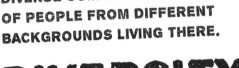

FACT

DIVERSE COMMUNITIES HAVE LOTS OF PEOPLE FROM DIFFERENT BACKGROUNDS LIVING THERE.

DIVERSITY

Equality is about treating everyone the same and being fair. Diversity is about recognising and celebrating people's differences. For example, allowing people to celebrate whatever holidays they like is an example of equality. However, if the community got involved and helped everyone celebrate each of their holidays, this would be an example of celebrating diversity. Then everyone gets to celebrate together.

Diversity is the belief that it is important to have different cultures in a community. It is also the belief that people should help immigrants to hold on to their lifestyle and culture. Diversity is very important. It helps immigrants feel welcome and makes our communities more interesting places to live. Without diversity, our communities would all be the same. This would be really boring.

Immigration brings people of different cultures together. We often find we are not as different as we thought, and that we actually have lots in common. We might also have lots of differences. This is a good thing. These differences can help make a community more interesting and exciting. If migrants in the past had never moved between countries, sharing ideas about food, music and clothing, the world today would be completely different. Nowadays, immigrants still do this – they help to bring new ideas to a community, which can help it grow and become more exciting.

FACT . . . .

MIGRATION CAN BRING EXCITING THINGS TO OUR COUNTRIES. IF WE HAD NEVER HAD IMMIGRATION FROM ITALY, WE MAY NEVER HAVE DISCOVERED PIZZA!

IMMIGRATION IN THE PAST

Around 100,000 years ago, all humans lived in the east of Africa. Today, humans live on almost every part of the planet. This change was only made possible through migration. Eventually, humans had finally spread to every **habitable** piece of land on the Earth – the last place to be reached was New Zealand. However, since this time there have been a number of important migration events.

EVERY SINGLE HUMAN BEING USED TO LIVE IN THIS AREA OF AFRICA.

FACT

A MIGRATION EVENT IS ANY TIME IN WHICH LOTS OF PEOPLE ALL MOVE FROM ONE PLACE TO ANOTHER, USUALLY BECAUSE OF STRONG, SUDDEN PUSH FACTORS.

IRISH POTATO FAMINE

Between 1845 and 1852, Ireland experienced a famine. A famine is a time when food is very difficult to find, meaning that many people go hungry and die. The famine in Ireland started when most of the potato plants in the country died. In order to escape the famine, around one million people emigrated from Ireland. Most of these people became immigrants in the United States of America.

IRELAND

USA

FACT

TODAY, OVER 30 MILLION PEOPLE IN THE U.S.A. ARE OF **Irish descent**. IRELAND ITSELF IS ONLY HOME TO AROUND SIX MILLION PEOPLE.

WORLD WAR II

People who follow the religion Judaism are known as Jewish. During World War II, millions of Jewish people were persecuted, attacked, put in prison and killed. This was done by Adolf Hitler and his Nazi government in Germany.

PALESTINE

ISRAEL

Today, this is known as the Holocaust and many people see it as one of the worst events in human history. The holocaust caused lots of Jews to emigrate from countries in Europe in order to escape persecution and death.

THIS IS TEL AVIV, THE LARGEST CITY IN ISRAEL.

Many Jewish people emigrated from Europe to the United States of America. However, many also moved to an area of the Middle East known today as Israel. Soon after the war, Israel became a country and it became a safe place for Jewish people to migrate to.

THIS IS THE FLAG OF ISRAEL. IN THE CENTRE OF THE FLAG IS THE STAR OF DAVID – AN IMPORTANT SYMBOL IN THE JEWISH RELIGION.

FACT . . . .

THERE ARE AROUND 15 MILLION JEWS IN THE WORLD TODAY. AROUND 6 MILLION JEWS, OR 40% OF ALL THE JEWS IN THE WORLD, LIVE IN ISRAEL.

CASE STUDY: SYRIAN REFUGEES

Since 2011, there has been a terrible civil war in Syria. There is often fighting in the streets and many towns and cities in Syria have been destroyed. Many Syrian people have tried to avoid danger by leaving the country, which has led to a migration event. Because these people have had to leave their homes suddenly and do not have anywhere to go, they have become refugees.

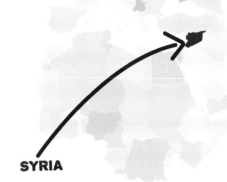

SYRIA

Since the war began, over five million Syrians have emigrated from their country as refugees. Many of these people had to walk tens or hundreds of miles to escape the fighting, taking only a few possessions with them.

THESE SYRIAN REFUGEES ARE WALKING TO TURKEY TO ESCAPE THE CIVIL WAR.

More than five million people have left Syria as refugees. Nearly three million of them now live in Turkey. About 30% of these people live in huge refugee camps that were specially made to give refugees from Syria somewhere to live. These camps are not perfect and are only temporary, but they have helped thousands of refugees who had nowhere else to go. The rest of the Syrian refugees in Turkey live in towns and cities.

TURKEY

SYRIA

TURKEY HAS SPENT BILLIONS OF POUNDS HELPING REFUGEES FROM SYRIA.

LEBANON

SYRIA

After Turkey, the country that is home to the most Syrian refugees is Lebanon. Over a million refugees have emigrated to Lebanon since 2011. Because Lebanon is such a small country, the Syrian refugees now make up 15% of its population.

FACT  . . . .

MIGRATION EVENTS CAN BEGIN AT ANY TIME. BECAUSE OF THIS, IT IS IMPORTANT THAT WE ALL LEARN TO BE WELCOMING AND ACCEPTING.

IMMIGRATION TODAY

For the last few decades, the number of people migrating has continued to rise. This is partly because migrating has become much easier and cheaper, thanks to better technology and transportation. Today, there are more immigrants than ever before, with roughly 250 million immigrants worldwide. This means that around one in every 30 people is an immigrant.

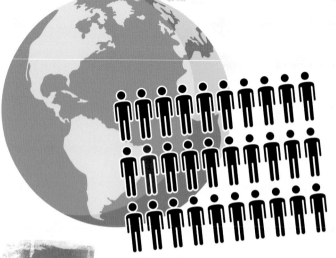

FACT . . . .

EUROPE IS HOME TO AROUND ONE-THIRD OF ALL THE IMMIGRANTS IN THE WORLD.

FACT  . . . .

THIS IS BERLIN, THE CAPITAL CITY OF GERMANY. GERMANY IS HOME TO MORE IMMIGRANTS THAN ANY OTHER COUNTRY IN EUROPE.

FACT . . . .

THE UNITED STATES OF AMERICA IS HOME TO AROUND 20% OF ALL IMMIGRANTS.

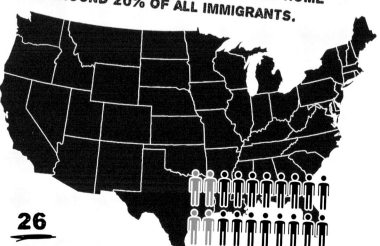

FACT . . . .

16 MILLION PEOPLE FROM INDIA HAVE EMIGRATED TO OTHER COUNTRIES – MORE THAN FROM ANY OTHER COUNTRY IN THE WORLD.

Migration means countries and communities will continue to become more diverse, with more and more people from different backgrounds and places coming together. For many people, this is something to celebrate and an opportunity for all of us to experience more of the world.

Migration is a part of every country in the world and more and more people decide to move to a new country every year. In order for communities to grow and for people to work together, we all need to be welcoming of others.

IMMIGRATION AND POLITICS

Politics is the name given to describe the actions and decisions of governments. Part of politics is deciding a country's laws, including the laws about who can migrate to the country. Because of this, governments and politics can greatly affect how people move between different countries.

In recent years, lots of governments have begun to wonder whether their immigration laws should be changed to make it harder for people to migrate to their country. This is because some people are worried that there won't be enough money, houses or jobs for everyone.

Because of this, countries make rules about who can immigrate and who can't. However, countries often want people to immigrate too. For example, if a country doesn't have enough doctors they might make rules that make it easier for doctors from other countries to immigrate.

It is also important to remember that, even if lots of people migrate to a country, lots of people may also emigrate. This helps the number of people living in the country remain well-balanced so there is still plenty of money and jobs to go around.

The European Union (EU) is a group of 28 European countries that decided to work together. The EU makes it easy for people in EU countries to immigrate to and trade with other EU countries. However, in June 2016, the UK decided to leave the EU. This will make it harder for people to immigrate to and emigrate from the UK.

FIND OUT MORE

TO FIND OUT MORE ABOUT TOPICS RELATED TO IMMIGRATION AND TOLERANCE, CHECK OUT THE LINKS BELOW.

To find out more about refugees
around the world, visit:
http://www.roads-to-refuge.com.au

To learn more about the history and
meaning of tolerance, visit:

https://www.learningtogive.org/resources/teaching-tolerance

GLOSSARY

civil war fighting between different groups of people in the same country

community a group of people who live and work in the same area, or share similar values & beliefs

conflict active disagreement between people

culture the traditions, ideas and ways of life of a particular group of people

economic to do with the way trade and money is controlled and used by a country or region

foreign born in, belonging to, or characteristic of some place or country other than your own

governments the group of people with the authority to run a country and decide its laws

habitable capable of being lived in

Irish descent when your parents or ancestors are from Ireland

laws rules that a community recognises as having authority

nationality the country that a person is from

possessions things that belong to a person

race a group of people who share the same culture, history or ethnicity

resources useful things

services supplying things that people need, such as power or transport, to a community

social relating to a group of people or a community

technology machines or devices that are made using scientific knowledge

traditions related to behaviours or beliefs that are part of a long-established custom

transportation vehicles used for moving goods or people around

tsunamis very large waves caused by an earthquake

INDEX

PHOTO CREDITS